KU-451-680

501
THINGS TO FIND

igloobooks

INTRODUCTION

Welcome to the exciting world of Joey JCB and all his JCB friends.
Follow the team around lots of fun JCB scenes and see if you can
find the hidden characters in each. Once you've found them,
see if you can find all the other hidden items as well.

Joey JCB

Larry Loadall

Elvis Excavator

Rex Roller

Max

Doug Dumptruck

Tommy Truck

Dan Dozer

Marty Mixer

Freddie Fastrac

Roxy Robot

Practise your JCB spotting skills and see if you can
find all 11 JCB friends on the opposite page?

PRACTICE SITE

When you've found these items, you're ready to go!

3 JCB flags

5 green barrels

7 red tyres

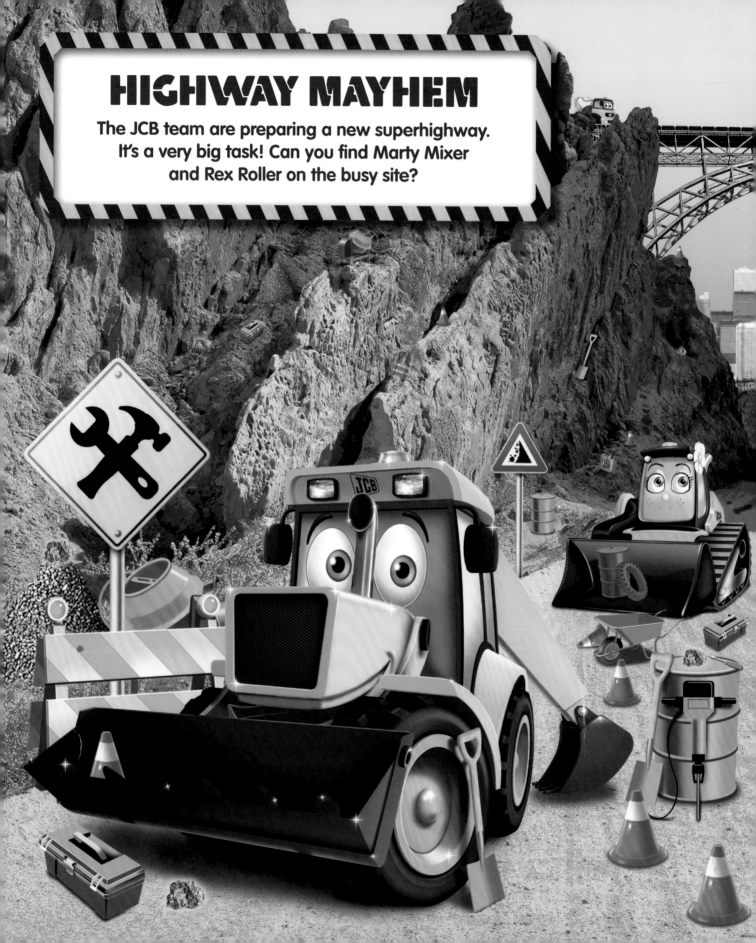

HIGHWAY MAYHEM

The JCB team are preparing a new superhighway.
It's a very big task! Can you find Marty Mixer
and Rex Roller on the busy site?

Can you spot these things, too?

1 crane

3 cement mixers

4 piles of rubble

6 toolboxes

8 spades

15 gold nuggets

RALLY RACES

It's the annual JCB rally and the team are racing around the muddy track. Try to find Max and Tommy Truck in the high-speed action.

Great! Can you find these items, too?

1 JCB trophy

3 chequered flags

4 muddy puddles

6 JCB flags

8 racing helmets

10 red tyres

What a race!
Who do you
think is
going
to win?

BUILD IT UP

Joey and his JCB friends are busy on a high-rise
building site. Can you spot Elvis Excavator and
Roxy Robot working hard somewhere up high?

Now can you find all these items, too?

1 red oil drum

3 blue crates

4 jackhammers

7 cement bags

8 warning signs

10 hard hats

FARMYARD FUN

The JCB team are helping out on Mr Bamford's farm. Search the scene and try to find Doug Dumptruck and Tommy Truck working hard.

Well done! Can you find all of these things, too?

1 combine harvester

3 piles of straw

4 chickens

6 blue wheelbarrows

8 pitchforks

10 bags of feed

What a noisy place! Who is loading feed into the barn?

QUARRY CHAOS

It's a busy day at the quarry, as the JCB friends move and sort all the different materials. Can you spot Marty Mixer and Larry Loadall on the messy site?

Can you spot these things, too?

1 diamond

3 blue pipes

4 piles of debris

6 cones

8 pickaxes

15 yellow bricks

REST AND REPAIR

The JCB team have come back to JCB HQ to relax and get cleaned up. Where are Dan Dozer and Larry Loadall relaxing?

Now try to find these items, too.

1 hose

2 red petrol cans

4 buckets of water

6 spanners

8 JCB banners

15 spare wheels

Not everyone gets to rest. Which JCB friends are missing?

BRIDGE BUILDERS

Team JCB are hard at work building a new bridge.
Can you spot Joey JCB and Freddie Fastrac
on the busy construction site?

READY FOR TAKE-OFF

The JCB team are at an airport to repair the runway.
Hidden among the planes and luggage are
Dan Dozer and Rex Roller. Can you find them?

Great!
Now try to
find these
items, too.

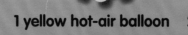

1 yellow hot-air balloon   2 luggage trolleys   4 red barriers

6 moving stairs

8 windsocks

15 blue suitcases

Up, up and away!
Who is loading
a special
engine onto
Tommy Truck?

IN THE FOREST

The JCB friends are busy replanting and restoring the forest. Hidden among the trees somewhere are Joey JCB and Doug Dumptruck. Can you find them?

Now try to find all of these things, too.

1 tree shredder

3 cabins

4 piles of sawdust

7 bags of seeds

8 red leaves

10 trees

FUN AT THE FAIR

What a hard day's work! Now it's time to relax and have some fun. Can you spot all 11 JCB friends having fun at the JCB theme park?

Excellent! Now try to find all these things, too.

1 JCB slide

2 cameras

4 signposts

7.6 BILLION PEOPLE LIVING IN THE COUNTRIES OF THE WORLD

CONTENTS

COUNTING DOWN THE WORLD'S CONTINENTS AND COUNTRIES

The Earth is made up of **seven** huge landmasses, called continents. These continents are divided into **195** countries. Within these countries live the **billions** of people, plants and animals that make up life on Earth. These huge numbers can be hard to imagine. Counting down the things on Earth helps to make sense of them.

COUNTING DOWN THE CONTINENTS

This book counts down the **seven** continents from largest to smallest.

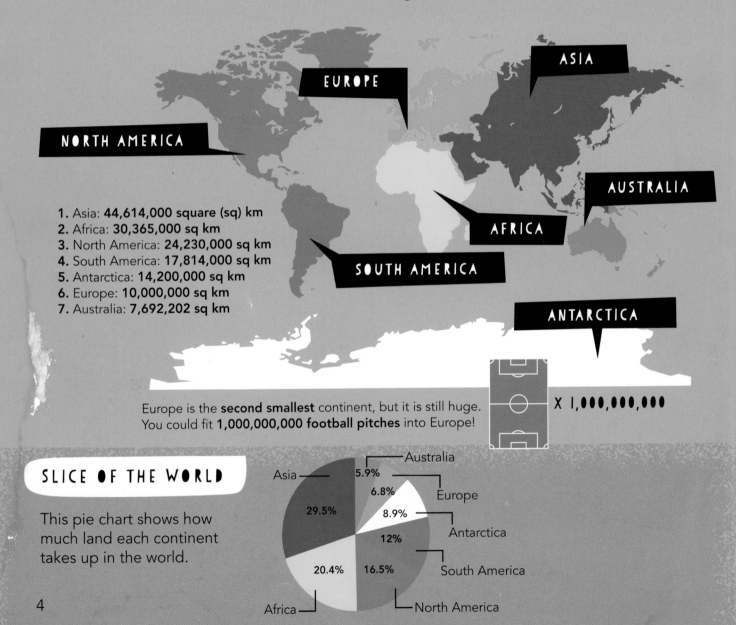

1. Asia: **44,614,000 square (sq) km**
2. Africa: **30,365,000 sq km**
3. North America: **24,230,000 sq km**
4. South America: **17,814,000 sq km**
5. Antarctica: **14,200,000 sq km**
6. Europe: **10,000,000 sq km**
7. Australia: **7,692,202 sq km**

Europe is the **second smallest** continent, but it is still huge. You could fit **1,000,000,000 football pitches** into Europe!

X 1,000,000,000

SLICE OF THE WORLD

This pie chart shows how much land each continent takes up in the world.

Asia — 29.5%
Australia — 5.9%
Europe — 6.8%
Antarctica — 8.9%
South America — 12%
North America — 16.5%
Africa — 20.4%